SPORTS HEROES AND LEGENDS™

Hank Aaron

Read all of the books in this exciting,
action-packed biography series!

Hank Aaron
Barry Bonds
Joe DiMaggio
Tim Duncan
Dale Earnhardt Jr.
Lou Gehrig
Derek Jeter
Michelle Kwan
Mickey Mantle
Jesse Owens
Ichiro Suzuki
Tiger Woods

SPORTS HEROES AND LEGENDS™

Hank Aaron

WITHDRAWN

by Serena Kappes

Lerne y/Minneapolis

*To my love—your encouragement is
a beacon of light in my life.*

Lerner Publications Company
A division of Lerner Publishing Group
241 First Avenue North
Minneapolis, MN 55401 U.S.A.

Website address: www.lernerbooks.com

Cover photograph:
© Bettmann/CORBIS

Library of Congress Cataloging-in-Publication Data

Leigh, David S., 1970–
      Hank Aaron / by David S. Leigh.
          p.   cm. — (Sports heroes and legends)
      Includes bibliographical references and index.
      ISBN-13: 978-0-8225-3069-5 (lib. bdg. : alk. paper)
      ISBN-10: 0-8225-3069-4 (lib. bdg. : alk. paper)
      1. Aaron, Hank, 1934– —Juvenile literature. 2. Baseball players—
United States—Biography—Juvenile literature. I. Title. II. Series.
      GV865.A25L45 2006
      796.357'092—dc22   2005002854

Manufactured in the United States of America
1 2 3 4 5 6 – JR – 11 10 09 08 07 06

Contents

Beyond Babe

On April 8, 1974, the Atlanta Braves played their home opener against the Los Angeles Dodgers. But this was no ordinary game.

Hank Aaron, the Braves' star right fielder, was attempting to break a record that had long been considered unbreakable. He was going to surpass Babe Ruth's career home run record of 714. This was about as big an event as baseball had ever seen, and Atlanta Stadium was filled beyond capacity. All 53,775 fans buzzed with excitement.

Some of the most important people in Aaron's life had come to witness the historic moment. Aaron's father, Herbert Aaron, threw out the first ball. His mother, Estella, sat anxiously in the stands. Famous entertainer Sammy Davis Jr. had flown in for the event. And Georgia governor Jimmy Carter had turned up to see Aaron swing with all his might.

Hammerin' Hank had his first at bat in the second inning. Dodgers left-handed pitcher Al Downing intentionally walked him. Then, in the fourth inning, with two outs and teammate Darrell Evans on first base, Hank readied himself to face Downing once again. The pitch was a low slider—just what Hank wanted to see. He made contact with the ball and slugged it toward deep left-center field. Dodgers center fielder Bill Buckner raced to the outfield fence, but he didn't have a chance to catch it. The ball soared over the fence and bounced into the Braves' bullpen.

Hank had just become baseball's new home run king. As he started to round the bases, the reality of what had happened hit him. "I was in my own little world at the time," he recalled. "It was like I was running in a bubble and I could see all these people jumping up and down and waving their arms in slow motion. I remember that every base seemed crowded, like there were all these people I had to get through to make it to home plate. I just couldn't wait to get there."

When Hank finally made it to home plate, Braves relief pitcher Tom House, who had caught the now-famous ball in the bullpen, ran toward him. "Hammer, here it is!" he shouted. Hank Aaron had done what at one time had seemed unimaginable—he'd hit his 715th home run.

Before long, it seemed like the entire stadium had swallowed him up. His parents hugged him, and the crowd erupted in deafening cheers. Governor Carter had reached home plate, where he presented Aaron with a special Georgia license plate: HLA 715. Then the game was stopped for a ceremony to mark the occasion. The only words that Aaron, who had fought so much to reach this moment, could utter were, "Thank God it's over."

When the historic game ended, the Braves had bested the Dodgers, 7–4. Hank Aaron's life was forever changed. Telegrams came pouring in, and President Nixon called to congratulate him.

When he finally left the stadium, Hank headed home for a party in his honor, surrounded by the friends and family he so treasured. But he needed a moment alone to process what had just happened. He headed to a quiet spot to reflect on his achievement.

Hank knelt down to pray. "At that moment, I knew what the past twenty-five years of my life had all been about," he recalled. "I had done something that nobody else in the world had ever done. I didn't feel a wild sense of joy. I didn't feel like celebrating. I felt a deep sense of gratitude and a wonderful surge of liberation all at the same time. I also felt a stream of tears running down my face."

All the years of hard work, more than twenty years of professional baseball, all the pain and joy had culminated in this moment. Every home run he hit after this point would set a new record—one that belonged to him.

Chapter | One

Dreaming Big

Henry Louis Aaron was born on February 5, 1934, in Down the Bay, a section of Mobile, Alabama, populated mainly by African Americans. He was the third child of Herbert and Estella Aaron.

Henry's beginnings were very humble. When the Alabama Dry Dock and Shipbuilding Company needed Herbert, he was a boilermaker's assistant. He had to hold up sixty-pound steel plates while another worker riveted them to the ship. Henry's mother, a deeply religious woman, stayed at home with the children, but she occasionally helped make ends meet by cleaning other people's houses.

The Aarons lived at 666 Wilkinson, where Henry and his older siblings, Herbert Jr. and Sarah, had been born. But by the time Henry was eight years old, the family—which expanded to include three more children—needed more space.

The Aaron family relocated to a nearby rural area called Toulminville. It was so rural that local pigs were the garbage pickup force. There, for the first time, the Aarons had their own home. Herbert Sr. bought two lots at $55 apiece and paid carpenters $100 to build a six-room house. The house wasn't fancy—it had no electricity, no windows, and no indoor plumbing—but the Aarons didn't mind. "We were a proud family," Henry said, "because the way we saw it, the only people who owned their own homes were rich folks and Aarons."

With the move came a sense of liberation. Toulminville had wide-open pastures filled with cows, chickens, hogs, watermelon patches, blackberry thickets, and more. The Aaron family literally lived off the land. They got their water from a well and gathered wood for cooking and heating the home.

HOMEGROWN TALENT

Hank Aaron wasn't the only future Hall of Famer from Mobile, Alabama. Chicago Cubs slugger Billy Williams and San Francisco Giants first baseman Willie McCovey also grew up there.

Meals were a simple affair. Cornbread, butter beans, and collard greens were the staples. The kids in the family described themselves as "six o'clock—straight up and down" because they were so skinny. "But we didn't feel sorry for ourselves," Henry explained, "because everybody was in the same boat."

As Henry grew older, he did odd jobs to help out with the family's expenses. He mowed yards, picked potatoes, and delivered ice. Years later, Aaron told sportswriters that he built up his famously strong wrists by hauling large blocks of ice up flights of stairs.

Young Henry found time to play baseball whenever he could. He had inherited his love of the game from his father, who ran a little baseball team out of the Black Cat Inn, a tavern Herbert Aaron had opened next to the family home. Henry was also inspired to play by his uncle Bubba (Estella's brother), a man whom he credits with teaching him about the game.

As a child, Henry had to finish his chores before he could go out to play baseball. He'd often show up after the game had already started. His friend Robert Driscoll explained that when any batter on the team saw Henry coming, he knew what to do. "Whoever was batting for our team, he would just lay that bat down on the ground," Driscoll explained, "because Henry was going to pinch-hit. . . . It happened to me many times."

Since times were tough and real baseballs were expensive, Henry would craft a ball by wrapping rags or nylon panty hose around old golf balls. Toulminville was a young baseball player's paradise, with acres of open fields where Henry and the other youngsters could play.

"Before long, enough kids had moved in that we could generally get up a game," Henry recalled. "After we had been there a few years, they cleared the pecan grove that was on the other side of a vacant lot across the street from my house, and we carved out our own ball diamond."

In 1945, after Toulminville became an official part of Mobile, that diamond and the surrounding land became Carver Park. It was the city's first recreational area for African Americans.

Henry practiced his game even when he couldn't find any other kids to play with him. He'd toss a ball onto the roof and run to the other side of the house to catch it before it landed on the ground. He also sharpened his reflexes by hitting tiny bottle caps with a stick.

Through his elementary school years, he never played an organized baseball game because his school, Toulminville Grammar School, didn't have a team. When he got to his high school, Central High, he was faced with the same situation. At the time, schools were segregated and only white schools had baseball teams.

Segregation was so pervasive that Henry rarely came into contact with white children. Once in a while, young African American and white kids would play together on an out-of-the-way field, but they'd have to make sure the police didn't spot them. They could get in big trouble just for being on the same field. In fact, Henry later said, "as a rule, black people in Mobile didn't know white people unless they worked for them."

Negro League baseball was founded around 1867. Some of the league's top players, including Satchel Paige, Cool Papa Bell, and Josh Gibson, were later inducted into the National Baseball Hall of Fame.

Henry had dreams of playing in the major leagues, but when he spoke to his father, Herbert told him that black people weren't allowed to play major league baseball. The only opportunity for an African American to play baseball professionally was in the Negro Leagues.

Since Henry's high school didn't have a baseball team, he played on his school's fast-pitch softball team. He was willing to try any position, including catcher, pitcher, and infielder. He reported that he hit a good number of home runs while playing in the all-black league. Coincidentally, his team was called the

Braves, named for one of Boston's two major league teams (the other team was the Red Sox).

Henry's talent on the field was obvious, but he also stood out because of a few unusual habits he'd developed at the plate. He waited until the last possible second to swing, and he swung with his weight on his front foot instead of his back foot. He also hit cross-handed—meaning as a right-handed batter, his left hand was on top when he gripped the bat. At nearby Hartwell Field, Henry would watch minor league teams like the Mobile Bears play. He noticed that nobody batted quite like him, but since his way worked for him, he didn't see a reason to change his style.

Baseball wasn't Henry Aaron's only sport. He also played football for several years. His mother was extremely upset when he quit the game in high school to focus exclusively on baseball. She believed education was important, and she'd hoped Henry could earn a college scholarship as a football player. (Colleges didn't offer the same sort of scholarships for baseball players.)

Hank's high school principal, Dr. Benjamin Baker, once chased him down the hallway with a cane because he was so upset that the promising young football player had quit the team.

Henry's baseball dreams got even bigger in 1947, when Jackie Robinson broke the major league color barrier. He joined the Brooklyn Dodgers to become the first African American major leaguer. Before long, Henry was so focused on baseball that school took a backseat.

In his third year of high school, he was expelled because he had skipped forty days of class in a row to go to the local pool hall. There, he could listen to the Brooklyn Dodgers games on the radio. "School couldn't teach me how to play second base like Jackie Robinson. I could learn that better by listening to the Dodgers on the radio. So that's what I did," he recalled.

Of course Henry didn't tell his parents that he was no longer enrolled as a student. But his father still figured out what was going on. One afternoon Henry's blissful escape into the world of major league baseball came to a crashing halt when Herbert walked into the pool hall. His paradise had been discovered.

After a long talk, Henry's father made him promise that he would go back to school. Herbert explained that his education was too important to let it fall by the wayside. "You can still be a baseball player," he told Henry. No longer welcome at Central High, Henry enrolled at the private Josephine Allen Institute for the following fall.

In the meantime, Henry devoted much of his time to playing at nearby Carver Park. Ed Scott, the manager of a local all-black semipro team, watched Henry play third base and invited him to join his team, the Mobile Black Bears.

&&*He said that every morning he put two quarters in my pocket so I could go to school and have a good lunch, and he only took one quarter with him to work, because my education was more important than his stomach.*&&

—HANK ON HIS FATHER, HERBERT AARON

Surprisingly, the invitation didn't make Henry happy. The team's home games were on Sundays, and his mother—a devout, churchgoing woman—would never allow him to play. That was a day for family and worship. Because Henry knew he'd never convince her, he avoided Scott.

Yet Scott refused to give up. After almost a month of visiting the Aaron home and pleading his case to Mrs. Aaron, Scott finally got his man. Estella made sixteen-year-old Henry promise that he'd return to school in the fall and only play in home games. Scott told Estella that Henry would earn ten dollars a game—no small amount for a teenager in 1950.

Every Sunday after that, Henry played shortstop for the Mobile Black Bears. In the field, he looked young, gangly, and inexperienced. But when he reached the plate, his bat told a completely different story.

"He stood up there at the plate upright, no crouch at all, and the other team figured he wasn't ready," Scott reported. "The pitcher tried to get a fastball by him, and he hit a line drive that banged against the old tin fence they had around the outfield out there—nearly put the ball through the fence." The opposing pitcher didn't take any more chances with Henry. He walked him for the rest of the game.

Henry still dreamed of the major leagues, but he had no reason to complain about his position with the Bears. "To me," he said, "it seemed about as good as it could get for the time being."

Chapter Two

Making His Mark

In the fall of 1950, Henry left the Mobile Black Bears. He made good on his promise to return to high school and entered the Josephine Allen Institute.

The following spring, Aaron resumed playing with the Bears. At this point, he became known as such a strong hitter that Scott, the team's manager, called his friend McKinley "Bunny" Downs, the business manager of the Negro American League's Indianapolis Clowns. Scott told Downs to come to Mobile to check out his hot young player.

During the game, Downs watched as seventeen-year-old Henry had three base hits and nimbly covered the field as a shortstop. After the game, an impressed Downs approached Henry. He found out his age, that he was still in high school, and asked him if he always played shortstop. "I play anywhere they want me to play," was Henry's response. "That's a nice attitude.

How would you like to play for the Indianapolis Clowns?" asked Downs. "I don't see no reason why not," Aaron responded.

But he spoke too soon. Estella would never let him forgo his education to play baseball full-time. She insisted that he could not join the team until he graduated from school in June 1952. Like a dutiful son, Henry agreed to his mother's demands.

Downs wasn't deterred—he claimed he'd send a contract for Henry after he turned eighteen. But Henry was crushed. He was sure he'd just lost his chance to play professional baseball. "I figured I'd never hear from him again," he later recalled.

But in the summer of 1951, Henry heard some amazing news. The Brooklyn Dodgers, Jackie Robinson's team, were coming to Mobile for tryouts. Here was his shot at the majors! He knew he had to do everything in his power to catch the attention of the scouts.

❝_Those scouts should have looked me over and said to themselves, 'What is this boy going to look like in a couple of years, when he starts eating and sleeping right and playing the game right?'_**❞**
—HANK ON THE BROOKLYN DODGERS

But things didn't go according to plan. The Dodgers took one look at Henry and decided that he was too small. At six feet tall and only 150 pounds, he didn't look like a powerful athlete. Ultimately, Henry got lost in the shuffle at the auditions and failed to impress the Dodgers.

School wasn't going much better for him. He was preoccupied with wondering whether he'd ever hear from Downs again. At the end of each day, he'd race home from school to check the mailbox. But by the winter of 1952, Henry was sure Downs had just moved on.

Then, shortly after Henry's eighteenth birthday, a letter from Downs arrived. It was a contract for Henry to join the Indianapolis Clowns! His salary would be $200 a month.

Although Henry hadn't yet graduated from high school, he promised his mother he'd finish his schooling in the off-season. "I couldn't miss this chance. I knew that if I waited around for a white [baseball] scout to sign me, I might never get out of Mobile," he explained.

In May 1952, Henry left his home wearing hand-me-down clothes and carrying two sandwiches, two clean pairs of pants, and two dollars. He was to take a train to Charlotte, North Carolina, where he'd travel by bus to Winston-Salem, North Carolina, the Clowns' spring training site. Before he left, Bears manager Scott handed Henry an envelope to give to Downs.

Henry felt more than a little nervous. In fact, the eighteen-year-old, who was traveling by train for the first time, was

15

downright scared. His knees were knocking and he wondered if he'd made the right decision and if he'd be able to impress the Clowns once he arrived.

Henry never peeked inside the envelope Scott had given him. He later found out that the note to Downs simply said, *Forget everything else about this player. Just watch his bat.*

Henry's arrival at spring training was not well received by the other players. Every new player who joined the team meant that one of the older players might get cut from the squad. And with the integration of major league baseball, the Negro Leagues were not as popular as they'd once been. For the guys who were too old for a shot at the majors, the Negro Leagues were all they had.

Henry suffered his share of taunts. Players asked him if he got his glove from the Salvation Army and made fun of his worn-out shoes. He was the butt of all of their jokes.

CLOWNING AROUND

To live up to their name, the Indianapolis Clowns would do funny things on the field, like play an imaginary game of catch. Their catcher even sat behind home plate in a rocking chair for a couple of innings.

Yet Henry tried to stay positive. "I knew I loved to play baseball," he said. "And I had a feeling that I might be pretty good at it." As he soon learned, the life of a baseball player on the road was anything but glamorous. The Clowns played as many as ten games a week, often in eight or nine different towns. The team pretty much lived on their bus, except for Saturday nights, when they stayed in a hotel.

But the scrawny kid from Toulminville proved that he could hold his own. The young shortstop was hitting .400 and batted fourth in the lineup. He helped the Clowns win game after game. The team's owners knew they had a serious prospect in Henry. They also knew that they could get good money for him if they sold him to a major league team. In fact, several major league teams, including the New York Giants, had put scouts on Henry's trail.

Clowns owner Syd Pollock wrote a letter describing Henry to John Mullen, minor league director of the Boston Braves. Intrigued, Mullen sent scout Dewey Griggs to watch the Clowns play a May 25 doubleheader against the Memphis Red Sox in Buffalo, New York. In his scouting report, Griggs noted that Henry played well. "This boy could be the answer," he wrote.

But Griggs had a few concerns. He noticed that when Henry threw to first base, he tossed it underhanded or sidearm. Griggs wanted to see a quick, powerful throw. He also worried about Henry's cross-handed batting style.

After the first game of the doubleheader, Griggs approached Henry in the Clowns' dugout. "Can't you throw any better than that?" he asked Henry. "Oh, sure, I can throw any way you want it thrown. I just been throwing enough to get them out," Henry responded. Griggs advised Henry to stop batting cross-handed immediately, telling him, "You'll never be able to play in the big leagues. . . . Those pitchers will knock the bat right out of your hands."

Taking Griggs's advice to heart, Henry changed his batting style in the second game, and he even smacked a home run. His performance as shortstop was equally impressive.

Just to make sure Henry played well consistently, Griggs attended another doubleheader about a month later. After watching Henry rack up seven hits—including two home runs—in nine at bats, he was sure he'd found his new man.

Suddenly the Dodgers, who had earlier rejected Henry, became interested in him. Word had spread that Henry Aaron was a rising baseball talent. A bidding war broke out between the Dodgers and the Braves. The New York Giants began clamoring for him too. Henry ultimately decided to go with the Braves. They offered him a salary of $350 a month, $100 more than the Giants were offering him.

But Henry wouldn't play in the major leagues right away. He'd begin with a minor league team. As he proved himself, he would move up through the minor league ranks, eventually (he hoped) making it to the majors.

Because Hank was still so young when he signed with the Boston Braves, his father had to sign his contract too.

Once again, Henry was heading into unknown territory. He took his first-ever airplane flight in June 1952 to Eau Claire, in central Wisconsin. And yet again, Henry had a bad case of nerves. "I'll never forget that plane," he later said. "I was . . . bouncing around in the sky over a part of the country I'd hardly ever heard about, much less been to, headed for a white town to play ball with white boys."

The Braves wanted Henry to finish the 1952 season with the Eau Claire Bears of the Northern League, a Class C farm (minor league) team. For the first time, Henry would be playing on an integrated team. The only other African American players were catcher Julie Bowers and outfielder Wes Covington.

Henry's initial intimidation quickly turned to confidence. "When you hear all your life that you're inferior, it makes you wonder if the other guys have something you've never seen before," he recalled. "It didn't take long to find out that the ball was still round after it left a white pitcher's hand, and it responded the same way when you hit it with a bat." In his first game with the Bears, he hit two singles, and by his second week he'd slammed his first home run.

Despite his success on the field, Henry had a hard time adjusting off the field. He was very homesick and felt isolated. Two weeks after arriving in Eau Claire, he packed his bags and called his family to tell them he was coming home. Luckily, a phone conversation with his older brother, Herbert Jr., convinced him to stay put. Herbert told him not to give up on his dream of playing in the major leagues.

It's a good thing Henry stuck around. In mid-July he was picked as the shortstop in the Northern League All-Star game. By the end of his first season in the minors he was the league's second-leading hitter. His average was .336, and he had 9 home runs and drove in 61 runs in 87 games. He was also named the league's Rookie of the Year.

After the season's end, Henry went back to play with the Indianapolis Clowns in the Negro World Series. The team won the title in a best-of-thirteen-game marathon played in cities all over the South. Henry hit five home runs and batted over .400. And, once the Negro World Series was done, he kept his promise to his mother. Henry finished the year by completing his high school degree.

Henry was moving up in the baseball world. During 1953 spring training in Waycross, Georgia, he found out that he'd been assigned to the Class A Jacksonville Tars, who were in Jacksonville, Florida. The Tars were an all-white team in the Southern Atlantic (or Sally) League. Henry, who was only nineteen, would be one of the first African Americans to desegregate the league.

Aaron could hit anybody. And for a skinny kid, he was incredibly strong.

—FIREBALL COHEN, HANK'S TEAMMATE
ON THE INDIANAPOLIS CLOWNS

Henry learned that he'd also have to take on a new position to play with the Tars. Top-notch shortstop Felix Mantilla would be joining Henry on the team, so Henry became a second baseman. He didn't mind making the switch. But despite his success on the team—in their first game, Henry swatted the team's only home run—it was a tough time for him. Along with the other African American players on the team, he suffered abuse from pitchers and spectators, who shouted racist insults.

"We knew that we not only had to play well, but if we ever lost our cool or caused an incident, it might set the whole program back five or ten years," he recalled. In fact, Henry and the others couldn't even react when pitchers tried to hit them with a ball. "When the pitchers threw at us, we had to get up and swing at the next pitch."

Henry also experienced life as a second-class citizen in other ways. Although the league had become integrated, the South was still segregated. The African American players couldn't sleep in the same hotels as the white players or eat in the same restaurants. Their teammates would bring food out to them while they waited in the bus, or they'd eat in the restaurant kitchen. The black players spent the night in homes on the African American side of town. Luckily, the team's manager, Ben Geraghty, was kind and kept an eye on Henry and his fellow players. He always made a point to visit where they were staying to make sure they were comfortable.

Despite difficult times off the field, Henry was proving himself mightily on it. During his 1953 season, he topped the league in batting average (.362), runs batted in (125), runs scored in (115), base hits (208), total bases (338), and doubles (36) and finished second in home runs (22). He was also named to the Sally League's All-Star team and honored as the league's Most Valuable Player (MVP). "Henry Aaron led the league in everything but hotel accommodations," a local sportswriter wrote.

Integrating the Sally League also had an upside. African Americans turned out at the ballparks in droves to see the

22

African American players on the field. In many of the stadiums, the "colored section" had to be expanded to make enough room for all the fans.

Meanwhile, Henry's personal life was also going well. He asked Barbara Lucas, a college student he'd begun dating in Jacksonville, to marry him. Their wedding took place on October 6, 1953.

❝I had [T. C. Marlin] introduce me as one of the next great stars of baseball. I don't think she was impressed.❞

—HANK ON MEETING HIS FUTURE WIFE, BARBARA LUCAS

Henry and his new bride traveled together to Puerto Rico. There, Henry joined the Caguas team to play winter baseball in the Puerto Rican League. Quickly, the team realized that second base might not be Henry's best position. Why not try him as an outfielder? Good move. His stellar fielding and throwing skills made him a serious threat out there.

Henry faced a lot of major league talent in the Puerto Rican League. He realized for the first time that he had what it takes to play with the big boys. "I saw major league pitching almost every day, and after a while—and after I moved to the outfield—I began to hit it," he recalled.

At the season's end, he finished third in the league in batting average (.322) and tied for first in home runs (9). In addition, he was named MVP in the league All-Star game. He was ready to find out whether his hard work would pay off when he joined up with the Braves for spring training in 1954.

Chapter Three

Hammerin' Hank

In the spring of 1954, when Henry reported to Bradenton, Florida, he hoped to be promoted to the Braves' major league team, which had moved to Milwaukee, Wisconsin, the year before. But at first glance, there didn't seem to be a position available for Henry. On his arrival for spring training, it was clear that the outfield was already staffed with experienced players—Bill Bruton, Andy Pafko, Jim Pendleton, and the newly acquired Bobby Thomson. Aaron had a sinking feeling that he had nowhere to go. He told Barbara not to put away the suitcases—he was sure he'd have to leave for the minor leagues at any moment.

Then a twist of fate intervened. On March 13, in an exhibition game against the New York Yankees in St. Petersburg, Florida, Bobby Thomson fractured his ankle sliding into second base. Henry watched as Thomson was carried off the field.

The next day in practice, Henry had no idea what would happen. Manager Charlie Grimm walked up to him, tossed him a glove, and said, "Kid, you're my left fielder. It's yours until somebody takes it away from you." That was the official start of Henry's major league career.

When Hank first reported for duty with the Milwaukee Braves in 1954, his last name on his locker was misspelled Arron.

After spring training, the Braves went on a preseason barnstorming tour with the Dodgers, stopping off to play games in cities including Mobile, Alabama; New Orleans, Louisiana; Birmingham, Alabama; Memphis, Tennessee; Louisville, Kentucky; and Indianapolis, Indiana. In Mobile Henry got to play in front of his biggest fans—his family.

He proudly wore his Braves uniform—he was number 5—as he shared the field with Jackie Robinson. "I hoped my father remembered what I told him when I was fourteen," Henry said, "that I would be in the big leagues while Jackie was still there."

As Henry would soon learn, life wasn't any simpler as a black man in the majors than it was in the Sally League. But during the barnstorming tour, he was able to learn from his idol, Robinson, and the other African American Dodgers. The black players spent lots of time together since they had to stay in separate hotels, segregated from the white players on the teams. "Those hotel rooms were my college," Henry recalled. The players talked about prejudice, how to deal with racist fans, and how they had to rise above racism. It was an eye-opening experience for Henry.

The "college student" and newlywed was experiencing other new worlds as well. Twenty-year-old Henry had become the father of Gaile Aaron. It wasn't easy being away from his new baby girl while on the road (she stayed with his parents in Alabama), but he was excited to make his major league baseball dreams come true.

On the field, Hank—as his teammates had nicknamed him—wasn't quite playing to the best of his ability. In his first game as an official major leaguer, he went hitless against the Cincinnati Reds. But two days later, on April 15, 1954, he hit a double off pitcher Vic Raschi of the St. Louis Cardinals. On April 23, in the fourth inning of another game against the Cardinals, he slugged his first major league home run. By the end of the season, he hit twelve more. "Once I got acclimated, I found that playing in the big leagues wasn't nearly as hard as getting there," he commented.

But Hank's first season in the majors ended early when he slid into third base during a game in early September. The slide broke his ankle. His end-of-season stats showed a .280 average, 13 homers, and 69 runs batted in (RBIs). And sadly, the Braves—who had caused a huge stir for Milwaukee baseball fans excited to have a team to call their own—finished the season in third place in the National League, behind the Giants and the Dodgers.

During the off-season, with his leg in a cast, Hank and Barbara headed back to Toulminville. Hank focused on his recovery, and once the cast was off, he was all business. He and his younger brother, Tommie, who was just fifteen at the time, would head down to his old stomping grounds, Carver Park, for batting practice.

By the time spring training rolled around in 1955, Hank's ankle had healed and he had a new set of goals. He wanted to play well in his sophomore year as a major leaguer and hit .300. He reported for training early and showed that his diligent off-season workouts had paid off.

Hank has always been a big film fan. In his early days on the road, if he had time off, you'd find him at a movie theater.

Bobby Thomson had also recovered and was back in the lineup, and the coaches moved Hank over to right field. With that change, Hank asked for a new uniform number—44. It commemorated the four positions he'd played in the previous four years. When he first asked the team's traveling secretary, Donald Davidson, for the two-digit number, Davidson jokingly replied that he was too skinny to carry around two numbers. But he eventually gave in to Hank's request.

In 1955 Hank showed that despite his slim build, he could certainly handle the weight of his numbers. A hot first half of the season earned him his first appearance in the All-Star game. He went 2 for 2 (2 hits in 2 at bats) as the National League won 6–3. By season's end, he'd batted .314, hit 27 homers, had 106 RBIs, and was named the team's MVP. Unfortunately, the team finished the year in second place. They just couldn't seem to surpass those amazing Dodgers.

During the 1955 season Hank also earned his new nickname—Hammerin' Hank. A New York sportswriter used the name in a newspaper column that mentioned one of Hank's home runs. Team traveling secretary Davidson liked the sound of it, and he convinced others to start using the nickname.

With the end of that year's baseball season, it wasn't quite time for a break. Hank joined up with a group of African American major leaguers, including Don Newcombe of the

Dodgers and Willie Mays of the Giants, on a barnstorming team. They played against a team of Negro League All-Stars. On the road, Hank got to know Mays, who had joined the Giants in 1951. It was an incredible experience. "We didn't lose. I mean we didn't *ever* lose," Hank later boasted. "That might have been the best team ever assembled. I know I never saw a better one."

Playing with the team also gave Hank a financial boost. He earned several thousand dollars for the tour. And for the 1956 season, Hank's salary was increased to $17,000, which he negotiated from the $13,500 the Braves offered him originally.

When Hank showed up for spring training in 1956, he was eager to play. "Ol' Hank is ready," he announced after his first batting practice of the season.

That was certainly true. The team hit a rough spot early on when manager Charlie Grimm was replaced by Fred Haney. But by June the Braves had an eleven-game winning streak and landed in first place. The Milwaukee fans couldn't get enough of the team.

"The whole state became excited about the Braves," Hank reported. "There were Braves hairdos and Braves cocktails and Braves banners stretched across the streets. Everybody thought we'd make it to the World Series, including the players." To make it to the World Series, the Braves would have to win the league pennant by finishing the season with the best record in the National League.

It wasn't meant to be. On the last weekend of the season, the Braves fell one game behind the Dodgers, finishing the season with a 92–62 record. Hank looked for the positive in the team's second-straight second-place year—it was Jackie Robinson's last year in baseball. Hank believed that it was only right that Robinson should end his career by playing in the World Series.

Hank, for his part, had accomplished his own personal goal. He ended with a .328 batting average. He also became the second-youngest batting champion (the player with the highest regular season batting average) in National League history. To top it off, Hank surpassed the twenty-homer mark for the second season in a row, and he led his league in hits (200) and doubles (34). And *The Sporting News* named him National League Player of the Year.

❝*I think the umpires liked me, because I made their job easy. I would swing at anything in the area code, and I never argued.*❞

—HANK ON HIS EARLY YEARS WITH THE BRAVES

Importantly, he was learning to truly trust his instincts at the plate. Hank would stay up nights thinking about the pitcher he'd face the next day, mentally preparing himself for whatever they might throw his way. His keen eyesight helped him as well. "Sometimes I could read the pitcher's grip on the ball before he ever released it and be able to tell what pitch he was throwing," he remarked.

Hank and his teammates wouldn't take no for an answer in 1957. After a grueling spring training, which felt more like boot camp, they were ready to fight all the way to the World Series. As the season began on April 16 at Chicago's Wrigley Field, Hank was in top form. The Braves beat the Cubs 4–1.

❝I never dreamed he would hit a bunch of home runs, because that wasn't the type of hitter he was. Henry was the type of hitter who would use the whole field.**❞**
—BRAVES PITCHER WARREN SPAHN

Hank's family had also moved to a pretty home in the country suburb of Mequon, Wisconsin. And Barbara gave birth to a son, Hank Jr., nicknamed Hankie. All around, it was a good time for the Aaron family.

By May Hank had been moved into the cleanup spot (fourth in the lineup). This spot is reserved for the team's best power hitter—someone the manager can rely on to drive in a lot of runs. And although Hank had never really considered himself a home run hitter, the year 1957 changed his mind. By the end of May, he'd already slammed twelve homers.

The team suffered some ups and downs during the season, but with the addition of second baseman Red Schoendienst to the Braves roster, the season took a turn for the better. Hank and his teammates said they believed that Schoendienst made the team complete.

The Braves still had to adjust to a few other changes in the course of the season. Hank sprained his ankle during a game that summer, but he was determined not to let his teammates down. After sitting out a few games, he came back to play center field because fellow outfielder Bill Bruton had collided with shortstop Felix Mantilla during a game. With Bruton out for the rest of the season, the team's confidence was shaken. But by early August, with sensation Bob Hazle joining the team from the minors, the Braves had muscled their way into first place.

BIG GAME

On September 2, the Braves faced the Chicago Cubs at Wrigley Field. The Braves pulled off their biggest win of the season that day, crushing the Cubs 23–10. Hank helped his team by driving in six runs.

On August 16, Hank swatted his thirty-third and thirty-fourth homers of the season in a game against Cincinnati. With his help, the Braves had a seven-game winning streak in September, though the St. Louis Cardinals were close on their heels.

On September 23, at 11:34 PM, Hank's team really needed his help. The Braves were playing the Cardinals and the game was all tied up, 2–2, in extra innings. At the bottom of the eleventh, when Hank stepped up to bat, his teammate Johnny Logan was on first. Hank knew that if he could get Logan home, the Braves would win the game and the pennant. Cardinals pitcher Billy Muffett was on the mound, and he hadn't given up a single homer all season long. But when Muffett threw a breaking ball his way, Hank walloped a home run beyond the center-field fence and into a grove of pine trees. Hank dashed around the bases and his teammates jubilantly carried him off the field. He later called that home run his greatest moment in baseball.

Yet even while celebrating his team's triumph, Hank couldn't escape the effects of racism. The cover story in newspapers the following morning described a mob of white protesters who tried to prevent nine African American students from entering, and desegregating, Central High in Little Rock, Arkansas. It was a sharp reminder to Hank that despite all of his success, African Americans still faced injustice across the country.

On September 24, Hank banged out his forty-fourth home run, a grand slam, off Sam Jones of the Cardinals. That hit won him his first home run title. His 132 RBIs also earned him the league RBI title. And Hank finished third in batting average with .322, behind Stan Musial and Willie Mays. If Hank had led all three categories, he would have won baseball's Triple Crown. But he was more excited about his team's chances in the 1957 World Series.

Chapter Four

Bushville Wins!

The New York Yankees were the clear favorites to win the 1957 World Series. The Yankees had already won seventeen world championships. The Braves—back when they were still in Boston—had won just one. New York felt so confident that they referred to the Braves as "bush leaguers," or minor league players.

But Hank and his crew refused to be intimidated by the Yanks' killer lineup, which included center fielder Mickey Mantle and catcher Yogi Berra. The Braves were determined to make their hometown proud in the Fall Classic.

Game one took place at Yankee Stadium and the Yanks won 3–1. Hank energized his team in game two by knocking a triple over Mantle's head. The Braves won 4–2.

Back in Milwaukee for game three, despite a homer by Hank, the Braves fell apart, losing 12–3. The Yanks had a 2–1 lead in the series. Game four looked good when Hank smacked a three-run homer in the bottom of the fourth inning. And with the Braves leading 4–1 at the end of the eighth inning, a win seemed certain.

❝Hank was a complete ballplayer. He never threw to the wrong base, never missed the cutoff man. . . . He could steal bases. He could run like hell, and he didn't even look like he was running.❞

—BRAVES TEAMMATE EDDIE MATHEWS

Milwaukee fans began filing out of the stadium as the Yankees came up to bat in the ninth inning. They were sure the game would be over in a matter of minutes. But with two runners on base, Elston Howard—the first African American player to join the Yankees—stepped up to bat. He knocked a home run right out of the park and tied the game. The Braves couldn't manage to score any runs in the bottom of the ninth. Then, a Hank Bauer triple helped the Yanks take the lead in the top of the tenth. But the Braves weren't ready to give up. Felix Mantilla scored on a Johnny Logan double to tie the game. Then third baseman Eddie Mathews hit a two-run homer and Milwaukee took the game, 7–5. "After that, we felt like we couldn't be beaten," said Hank.

The Braves took game five, 1–0, and returned to New York for game six. If they won, the series would be over. Milwaukee could see victory on the horizon—they just had to make it theirs.

Hank knew he had to do his part to make that victory a reality. He hit his third home run of the series in game six. It happened at the top of the seventh inning, and it helped tie the game, 2–2. Then, at the bottom of the seventh, Yankees outfielder Hank Bauer scored a run, giving his team a one-run lead and leading to their 3–2 victory over the Braves. Game seven in the series would determine whether the Braves could best the Yanks and become world champs.

Game seven was all about the Braves. Milwaukee took a 4–0 lead after just three innings of play. The Braves' starting pitcher Lew Burdette threw his third complete game of the series. Incredibly, it was his second shutout of the series, and the Braves won with a final score of 5–0. The team the Yankees had derided as "bush league" had become the best in baseball.

The town of Milwaukee seemed like it might just explode from all the excitement. In downtown Milwaukee, fans carried around banners that read *Bushville Wins!* So many people swarmed the streets that the *Milwaukee Journal* observed, "A bulldozer would have had a hard time getting through."

Hank had batted an amazing .393 for the series, though pitcher Burdette was named MVP. But Hank received his own award when he was crowned National League MVP. Twenty-three-year-old Hank was thrilled with the World Series win and the award. "It doesn't get any better than Milwaukee in 1957," he later said.

And soon, Hank would be a dad again. Barbara Aaron was pregnant, this time with twins. The twin boys, Gary and Lary, were born prematurely in the winter of 1957. Sadly, Gary died in the hospital.

During this time, Hank found solace in the friendship of a white Catholic priest, Mike Sablica. The two men also discussed their thoughts about the civil rights movement. As part of the movement, African Americans held protests and demanded the right to life, freedom, and equal treatment.

After Hank's World Series win, he was invited back to Mobile for Hank Aaron Day. He was even given a key to the city. "That was a proud day for all the black people of Mobile—a kid from Toulminville being honored by the mayor himself," Hank noted.

Of the ten Most Valuable Players in the National League in the 1950s, eight of them were African American players. The MVPs included Hank, Willie Mays, and pitcher Don Newcombe.

Hank was also invited to speak at an all-white men's club in Mobile. When he asked if he could bring his father along, the club said they couldn't allow it. "It was one thing for a black World Series hero to speak to their club," he commented, "but it was another thing to have his black daddy sitting with all the good white men in the audience." He canceled the engagement. Experiences like this made Hank want to challenge the injustices he saw around him.

As 1958 rolled around, Hank and the Braves were eager for another trip to the World Series. The regular season went well and the Braves became National League champions for the second year in a row. They won the pennant by eight games over the Pittsburgh Pirates.

Baseball slang terms for a home run include *bomb, dinger, dong, round-tripper, moon shot,* and *tater.*

And Hank, who was still batting cleanup, had a solid season. He finished with a .326 average, 30 home runs, and 95 RBIs. He made it into the All-Star game again and received his first Gold Glove—the award for the league's best fielder at his position—at the end of the season. The Braves made their way to the World Series to meet up with the Yankees for the second consecutive year. "The two of us were far and away the class of our leagues," Hank later said, "and we knew that if we could beat them twice in a row we would clearly establish ourselves as the best team in baseball."

The Braves won three of the first four games, and victory was within reach once again. Yet this time around there would be no World Series rings for the Braves at the end of the rainbow. The Yankees came back to win the final three games. Although Hank's batting average for the series was a solid .333, he'd hit no home runs and had only two RBIs in the course of those seven games. "What happened in that series," Hank said later, "was sort of a tip-off on what was about to happen to the Braves over a period of seasons."

But Hank came back hitting better than ever in the 1959 season. "I was seeing the ball so well that I stopped going to the movies for a while, because I didn't want anything to affect my eyes," he recalled. His focus and determination were paying off. In April he batted .508, and in May he was still above .450.

By September the Braves found themselves tied for first in the league with a familiar opponent—the Dodgers. But the Dodgers had moved away from Brooklyn after 1957, becoming the Los Angeles Dodgers. When the teams remained tied at the end of the regular season, they were forced to play a three-game playoff series. Hank and the Braves felt certain that their team could best the Dodgers. "As far as we were concerned, the hard part was over, because we had survived the pennant race and we were sure—everybody in Milwaukee was sure—that we were the superior team," Hank said.

The first playoff game took place at Milwaukee County Stadium and the Dodgers won 3–2. The Dodgers kept up the momentum and won the next game, which was held in Los Angeles, 6–5. The playoffs were over that quickly. "It still bothers me that we were only able to win two pennants and one World Series with the team we had," Hank later commented. "We should have won at least four pennants in a row. . . . I wish I knew what kept us from winning more."

In the fall of 1959, Hank agreed to be on the TV show *Home Run Derby*, in which two major leaguers competed head-to-head for homers. Hank didn't expect to do very well in the contest, but in each matchup, he came out on top. In the end, he received $30,000 (almost twice his Braves salary) for his appearances on the show.

Suddenly, Hank looked at hitting home runs in a different way. He realized that the home run guys attracted a lot of attention. A healthy competition began to develop between Hank and his Braves pal Eddie Mathews, and they soon had a good-natured battle with each other for home run supremacy on the team. "Henry and I had a friendly rivalry. He pushed me and I pushed him. Rivalries were important to us," Mathews observed.

Hank used some of his $30,000 earnings from *Home Run Derby* to buy his parents a grocery store in Toulminville.

During the 1960 season, the Braves finished second in the league to the Pirates, but Hank and Mathews had an impressive 79 home runs and 250 RBIs between them. On July 3, 1960, Hank hit his 200th career home run off Ron Kline of the Cardinals. He ended the season with a .292 batting average. Hank had also become a key base-stealer—his 16 steals were twice as many as he'd gotten the year before.

The year 1961 would bring other accomplishments. On June 8, during a game against the Cincinnati Reds, Hank and three of his teammates became the first four players ever to hit successive homers. Despite a potent lineup, the team fell to fourth place at the end of the season. "We had become power-heavy and pitching-poor," Hank later explained.

By the 1962 season, the Braves were well out of first place. But in Hank's personal life, things were good. Daughter Dorinda was born on February 5, Hank's birthday. And Hank's younger brother, Tommie—who had followed in Hank's footsteps as a baseball player—was promoted from the farm team to the Braves. "We were a couple of proud Aarons in those days," he recalled. But even *two* Aarons weren't enough to bring the team back to the top of the National League—the Braves finished the year in fifth place.

As the 1962 season came to a close, Hank had hit .323, had blasted 45 home runs, and knocked in 128 RBIs. "I felt more responsibility to hit more home runs," Hank revealed. The longest ball he ever hit came during that season, when he hammered one about 470 feet from home plate.

❝My father really believed in education. He always said that you could break something and never play again, and the only thing to fall back on would be our education. He always said you could fall off the same ladder you climbed up on.❞

—HANK'S DAUGHTER, GAILE AARON

Hank's power at the plate brought more money—he was earning $50,000 a year, which helped the Aaron family live comfortably. The family would watch television on their new color set or have barbecues on their patio. The patio was shaped like a baseball field—it had a fence around it, benches for the bullpen, and a barbecue pit in the center, where the pitcher's mound belonged. Those were happy years for the Aarons.

Chapter | Five

Going South

With the glory of the 1957 World Series long behind them, the early 1960s had become a tough time for the Braves. Many of the original players who'd helped lead the team to victory in 1957 were traded. "The problem was that while the old Braves were being sent away, we weren't replacing them with good young players from our farm team," Hank later said.

By 1963 a slew of key players, including Wes Covington and Felix Mantilla, had been shipped off to other teams. Unfamiliar youngsters filled the holes in the roster. "Faces seemed to change every week. Players came and went like livestock," Hank recalled. "With the exception of [pitcher Warren] Spahn, Mathews, and me, we had become a team of kids."

And the once super-loyal Braves fans had lost their enthusiasm for their home team. After several less-than-stellar seasons, they were no longer the fanatics they had once been, and it showed in the bleak attendance records. Also, the Washington Senators had recently moved to Minnesota, on Wisconsin's border, and become the Minnesota Twins. The Twins gave baseball fans in the Midwest another team to root for.

Even with the lack of enthusiasm for the Braves, Hank wasn't about to give up on his team—or his ability to play the game he loved. During the 1963 season, the Braves became what Hank called "a plodding team" and he was called upon to help quicken the pace on the field. Manager Bobby Bragan encouraged him to steal more bases, and he ended up being second in the league with 31 steals in 36 attempts.

❝*I was strictly a guess hitter, which meant that I had to have a full knowledge of every pitcher I came up against and develop a strategy for hitting him.*❞

—HANK AARON

Early in Hank's career, he'd been considered a lethargic player because he never put on an extra burst of speed unless it was absolutely essential. But during this period, critics began to admire Hank's ability to juice things up. "It broke down some of the prejudice toward me," Hank later said. He was impressive in other ways too, batting .319 and garnering 44 home runs and 130 RBIs by season's end. Yet despite his individual success on the field, the Braves finished the season in a dismal sixth place in the league.

In a time when African Americans continued their struggle for civil rights, Hank and other black ballplayers were proving their prowess on the field. In 1963 the top National League hitters in total bases—Hank, Willie Mays, Vada Pinson, Orlando Cepeda, and Bill White—were all nonwhite. (Total bases are determined by the sum of all bases reached by batters against a pitcher as a result of base hits. A single counts for one point, a double counts for two, a triple is three, and a home run is four. Only bases from safe hits count toward this total.)

"By 1963, black players were leading the National League in so many things that it made you wonder what the quality of baseball was like before Jackie [Robinson] joined it—and what the quality of Negro League baseball was like before Jackie left it," Hank said.

"*I wasn't able to participate in civil rights marches because of baseball, but I'm not sure I would have been much good in one anyway. I don't think I could have been passive in that situation. Getting kicked by a second baseman was a part of baseball . . . but getting kicked by a policeman might have been more than I could tolerate.***"**
—HANK AARON

During this time, Hank became involved in the civil rights movement in his own way, requesting that all members (regardless of their race) of the Braves stay together at the same hotel during spring training. He didn't want to cause a great uproar, but he wanted to play a part in making a difference. Hank later explained that if he'd taken part in a civil rights protest, major league officials might have become extremely upset, so he focused on doing what he could to improve conditions for African Americans in baseball.

Baseball was a unique forum for African Americans and whites in the United States in 1963. "There weren't many places in America where blacks and whites worked alongside each other, there were fewer places where the black man could make more money, and there were no places more visible than the big-league ball fields," Hank observed.

In 1964 rumors started churning that the Braves would be making a move to Atlanta, Georgia. The rumor seemed true when the city of Atlanta unveiled its plans for the construction of a major league ballpark, Atlanta Stadium.

After Braves executives confirmed that they did plan to relocate, Milwaukee County took action and got a court order to prevent the ball club from moving until it had finished its contract with Milwaukee County Stadium, which ended after the 1965 season. "For the players—and for the fans—it was horrible to see our team and our city going at each other in court, like a messy, bitter divorce. We loved Milwaukee, and none of us wanted to move," Hank said.

PEPSI, PLEASE

The city of Milwaukee was so upset that the Braves were abandoning them for Atlanta that local restaurants and bars stopped serving Coca-Cola. The soft drink company is headquartered in Atlanta.

But for many reasons, the change seemed necessary. Although Hank ended the 1964 season with a .328 average and 24 home runs, the team was in a major slump. They ended with an 88–74 record and finished in fifth place, behind the Cardinals, the Reds, the Philadelphia Phillies, and the Giants.

When the 1965 season began, the fans just didn't seem to care anymore. They weren't about to support the team, knowing they were about to desert them. "They stayed away from the ballpark in droves," Hank remembered.

It didn't seem to matter to the fans that the Braves began to perk up during the 1965 season. Hank had missed the first three weeks because of an operation on his ankle, but he was soon back and looking better than ever. In fact, he and teammate Eddie Mathews broke the National League record for most career home runs by teammates on May 2, 1965. Hank and Eddie had been playing together for eleven years. Hank's 368 combined with Mathews's 378 to make 746. "I was lucky to have Eddie for a teammate all those years," Hank later said. "There's no doubt that he made me a better player."

By August 1965, the Braves were within two games of the league-leading Los Angeles Dodgers. But sixteen losses in September—including three losses to the Dodgers—did nothing to improve the team's position in the league standings. Hank continued to play hard, though. On September 20, Hank hit his 398th career homer, the last home run ever hit by a Milwaukee Braves player in Milwaukee County Stadium. Sadly, only a few thousand people were in the park to watch Hank make his final homer for his team.

❝Any ballplayer missed something if he didn't play in Milwaukee during those thirteen years. It was something else. If you wanted a doctor or lawyer, you had to call the ballpark.❞

—WARREN SPAHN

Ultimately, the Braves ended the season in fifth place with an 86–76 record. It was the end of an era for baseball in Milwaukee. "To this day, whenever I'm in Milwaukee, I'm reminded that the people there still haven't gotten over the Braves leaving," Hank later commented. But at that moment, Hank and the team had to look ahead to their future in Atlanta.

Chapter Six

Eyes on the Prize

When Hank Aaron arrived to play ball in Atlanta Stadium for the 1966 season, he knew things were going to be different. In Milwaukee, he was a fan favorite. But in Atlanta, his race came into play as it had years earlier when he was part of the Sally League.

GO, LITTLE BRO!

Hank's younger brother, Tommie, was the first player on the Atlanta Braves to hit a home run at the new Atlanta Stadium. He hit it during an exhibition game before the start of the 1966 season.

Hank quickly realized that he had to come up with a plan. "I needed a decisive way to win over the white people before they thought of a reason to hate me. And I believed that the way to do that was with home runs," he concluded.

When Hank started his career with the Atlanta Braves, he had a .320 lifetime batting average, the highest of all active players. But a high batting average doesn't necessarily correspond with a lot of home runs. During the Braves' first home game on April 12, 1966, Hank didn't score a single run—much less a home run. In fact, his only accomplishment was being the first player to steal a base in Atlanta Stadium.

But before long, Hank was swinging for the fences once again. Immediately, Hank could feel something different in the air in Atlanta than in Milwaukee. "Atlanta was the highest city in the major leagues, as well as the hottest, and if you could get the ball into the air, there was a good chance that it wouldn't come down in the playing field," he said. In a warm climate like the southern city, the heat and altitude help give the ball lift (as opposed to a colder climate, where the ball can be "hard," which means it doesn't carry as well after it's hit).

The ball carried so well in Atlanta Stadium—and the players hit so many home runs—that the park soon earned the nickname "The Launching Pad."

Hank turned thirty-two years old that year. He decided he needed to give up his rather unrealistic goal of batting .400 and focus even more of his attention on hitting home runs. As he became familiar with his new home field, he seemed to be able to gauge exactly how far he needed to hit a ball to knock it just beyond the outfield fence. And it wasn't just at home where he was hitting homers: On April 20, he smacked his 400th career home run in Philadelphia's Connie Mack Stadium. He was only the eleventh player in baseball history to reach that mark.

By season's end, he was the National League's top home run hitter (44) for the third time in his career. His batting average, at .279, was slightly lower than he preferred. But he'd also won his fourth RBI crown (127) and the Braves, now on a streak of their own, had scored more runs than any team in the league. Yet the Braves finished the year in fifth place.

Despite the fact that Hank was growing comfortable on his new home field, his new hometown was another story. While the Aaron family had happily settled into a ranch house on two acres in southwest Atlanta, not everyone in town welcomed the baseball player and his brood.

"There was often a hate letter or two in the mail, and I was always concerned about Barbara and the kids being abused when they went to the ballpark," Hank recalled. "If nothing else, they would hear me being called some of the same names that had burned my ears thirteen years before in the Sally League."

Hank was no longer content to remain silent when it came to racial matters. During the 1966 season, he did an interview with a reporter from *Jet* magazine, a publication geared toward African Americans. Hank spoke openly about the way black baseball players were discriminated against "in salary, longevity, managing, the front office, everything." It was a bold move for Hank to discuss the subject so openly in a major magazine.

Hank was growing in other ways. In October, after the season had ended, he and several other major leaguers embarked on a seventeen-day visit to U.S. military troops stationed in the Southeast Asian country of Vietnam. At the time, U.S. soldiers were fighting alongside the South Vietnamese army against the North Vietnamese. "It was an eye-opening experience for somebody like me, who had never given a lot of thought to war," Hank said.

During the off-season, Hank also visited the White House and met President Lyndon B. Johnson. Hank said the experience "made me feel like I was finally in tall cotton." Not long afterward, Hank signed his first $100,000 contract. With his new salary, Hank was in the company of players like Willie Mays, Mickey Mantle, Sandy Koufax, and Don Drysdale.

But as happy as he was with his new financial terms, Hank was sad to learn that his old pal and fellow home run record breaker Eddie Mathews was being traded to the Houston Astros in January 1967. It was devastating to lose his trusted friend. "He was the only Brave to play in Boston, Milwaukee, and Atlanta. As far as I was concerned, he was Mr. Brave . . . a ballplayer's ballplayer [who] would do anything to win," Hank said.

With all the trades that had gone on since he first joined the Braves, Hank was the final remaining member of the old guard on the team. Without Mathews on board, the 1967 season wasn't a smooth one for the Braves. The team finished under .500—losing more than half of their games—for the first time since the Braves moved to Milwaukee in 1953. And Hank even had to face Mathews and the Astros, who trounced the Braves during a game in the 1967 season. "We didn't seem like the Braves anymore," Hank later lamented.

But Hank was determined not to let his own personal game slide. He won his fourth home run title, led the league in runs scored, and brought his average back over .300. "It was a season I was proud of, except for the fact that the Braves had fallen deep into the second division," he commented.

The Aaron family had a frightening experience in 1967. Their house caught fire. The family poodle was killed, and many of Hank's trophies were destroyed. But Hank's motto, "always keep swinging," helped him persevere. "Whether I was in a slump or feeling badly or having troubles off the field, the only thing to do was keep swinging," he said.

❝The real world made me hungrier and angrier than I had been as a young Milwaukee Brave. I wasn't content anymore to let other guys have all the fame and fortune.❞

—HANK AARON

During the 1968 season, Hank got the opportunity to forge a friendship with legendary Negro League pitcher Satchel Paige. Paige, who had gone on to play in the major leagues after his tenure with the Negro Leagues, was a bit short of qualifying for his major league pension when he had retired years earlier. After reading of his plight, Braves owner Bill Bartholomay brought sixty-two-year-old Paige on board briefly so that he could qualify for it. Although he didn't pitch any games (the Braves were afraid he would get hurt), he would still throw on the sidelines. Hank was thrilled to have a chance to get to know one of his idols. "Because he was the living symbol of Negro League baseball, I felt a special kinship with Satchel," Hank recalled. "After spending time with Satchel, I firmly believe that he may have been the greatest pitcher of all time."

Hank Aaron *(left)* and several other minor league players desegregated the Southern Atlantic League in 1953. The Jacksonville Tars' manager, Ben Geraghty *(right)*, treated all of his players well, and at the end of the season, Hank was named league MVP.

At age twenty, Hank became the Milwaukee Braves' full-time left fielder. As a rookie, he smacked thirteen home runs.

When Hank wasn't busy playing baseball, he spent time with his growing family. His son, Hankie, was born in the spring of 1957.

Hank became friends with Willie Mays *(left)*, when they played together on an African American barnstorming team. When this photo was taken, the two sluggers were tied for career homers, with 648 each.

This sequence shows Hank's 700th home run, hit on July 21, 1973. The pitcher was Ken Brett of the Philadelphia Phillies

Teammate Dusty Baker (No. 12) congratulates Hank (No. 44) after his 703rd home run.

Hank smacked his record-breaking home run—number 715—at Atlanta Stadium on April 8, 1974.

After the game in which he hit his 715th homer, Hank spoke with reporters. He faced intense pressure from the media and from fans during the final months of his quest to break the record.

Hank and his wife, Billye, stand with his plaque at the National Baseball Hall of Fame. The plaque reads, in part, "HIT 755 HOME RUNS IN 23-YEAR CAREER TO BECOME MAJORS' ALL-TIME HOMER KING. HAD 20 OR MORE FOR 20 CONSECUTIVE YEARS, AT LEAST 30 IN 15 SEASONS AND 40 OR BETTER EIGHT TIMES. ALSO SET RECORDS FOR GAMES PLAYED (3,298), AT BATS (12,364), LONG HITS (1,477), TOTAL BASES (6,856), RUNS BATTED IN (2,297)."

In 1968 Hank also passed several milestones of his own. On July 14, he hit his 500th career home run off Mike McCormick of the San Francisco Giants. In August, Hank became the first African American player to have his own night dedicated to him at Atlanta Stadium. But the team as a whole didn't have a stellar season that year: They finished with an 81–81–1 record.

At spring training for the 1969 season, Hank looked around and started feeling his age. He was only thirty-five, but in baseball years, he was beginning to feel old. "It put the idea of retiring into my head for the first time," he said.

Then a baseball writer named Lee Allen interviewed him and spoke to him about all the things he'd yet to achieve, including having a chance to make 3,000 hits, a goal Hank had once set for himself. "Allen explained to me that the fun would really start when I reached 3,000 hits, because from that point on I would be able to create my own niche in baseball history," Hank later recalled. "To somebody like me—having come along in a period when black players were only beginning to assume their rightful place in baseball—the chance to make history sounded like something worth pursuing with all of my resources."

In July 1969, Hank rocketed his 537th home run, putting him third on the all-time home run list, ahead of Mickey Mantle and trailing only Babe Ruth and Willie Mays (who was still playing). He finished the regular season with a .300 batting average. But he wasn't quite done with that year's baseball season.

The thing I'll always remember most about The Hammer was his ability to play with pain. Many times, he'd limp into the clubhouse like he could barely make it to his locker. . . . Then it would be time for the game to start, and he'd get up like there was not a thing wrong with him. He'd pound the ball and run the bases like a kid.

—BRAVES TEAMMATE DUSTY BAKER

For the first time in years, the Braves were in a pennant race, thanks to their 93–69 record. They won the National League's new Western Division and faced off with the Eastern Division champs, the New York Mets. The top team in each division played in the best-of-five-game playoff series to determine the winner of the National League pennant. Although Hank was suffering his share of physical problems, including painful bone chips and calcium deposits in his back, he was elated to be playing in the league championship series.

Ultimately, the Braves were swept by the Mets, losing three in a row, 9–5, 11–6, and 7–4. Hank batted .357 and homered in each matchup. "I noticed that people started to view me a little more sympathetically—and respectfully—after that playoff series," Hank said. "Maybe people saw me as the old man going up against destiny and giving it one more good shot." But Hank's glory days definitely weren't behind him.

Chapter | Seven

Mr. 3,000

In the Braves' 1970 home opener against the San Francisco Giants, Hank hit the first home run to land in the left-field upper deck of Atlanta Stadium. Afterward, a gold hammer was painted on the seat to commemorate the spot.

On May 17, Hank Aaron joined an exclusive club when he made his 3,000th career hit. The club had only eight other members in it at the time, including Ty Cobb and Stan Musial. Notably, Hank was the first African American player to join it. "Three thousand hits was a big deal and my first brush with fanfare," he said. "It even got me on the cover of *Sports Illustrated* for the second time in two years—after fifteen years without ever being on it. More than anything else, 3,000 hits is a testament to a player's staying power."

The hit happened during a doubleheader against the Cincinnati Reds in Cincinnati's Crosley Field. Stan Musial, who'd become a close friend of Hank's during their trip to Vietnam, even ran down to the field to congratulate him. "It was getting awfully lonely," Musial, who was the only other living member of the elite clique, told Hank.

Hank's history-making hit was a dribbling ball against rookie pitcher Wayne Simpson. Hank was happy that hit number 3,000 happened at Crosley Field. He had a lot of memories there—it was the park where he'd played his first major league game and where he'd broken his ankle. Hank also got his 3,001st hit in the game, and it happened to be his 570th home run.

66Not long after I got my 3,000th hit that year, Willie [Mays] got his. It was the first time I had ever reached a milestone ahead of him, and, frankly, it felt good.**99**

—HANK AARON

When Hank returned to Atlanta, the Braves threw him a celebration. And what a festive event it was. He received a French poodle, a year's supply of Coca-Cola (Atlanta is the company's hometown), and a golf cart with the number 44 emblazoned on it. But the best prize of all was the actual ball that he'd hit for number 3,000.

Hank ended the season with a .298 average, 38 home runs, and 118 RBIs. His career home run total was up to 592. Yet the good came with the bad. Despite his personal achievements, said Hank, "there was no chemistry on the team anymore. We fell all the way from the top of the division to fifth place, with a losing record." The Braves' record had dropped to 76–86.

Hank's personal life had also hit a rough spot. He and Barbara divorced in February 1971. It was a lonely time for Hank, who moved into the Landmark Apartments in downtown Atlanta. He was sad to no longer live full-time with his children, but he made sure to spend whatever free time he had with them.

❝*I figured the best thing I could provide my kids was opportunity, because that's what the struggle was all about.*❞

—HANK AARON

Hank knew that he had to get back to business with the start of the 1971 season. He suddenly found himself in the position to one day break Babe Ruth's career home run record of 714. Ruth, who enjoyed his best seasons with the Yankees in the 1920s, had been the first professional athlete to earn more money than the president of the United States. He was a swaggering crowd-pleaser whose on-field and off-field antics were legendary. Hank, by contrast, was a quiet, serious player.

Breaking Ruth's record was a tall order for thirty-seven-year-old Hank, but he set his sights on doing it. "This year and next year are going to be critical ones if I'm going to catch Babe Ruth," he said at the start of the 1971 season. "I'd almost have to hit fifty in one of those seasons, I think. I need to have a big year, I know that."

Hank began to get to know some of the younger players on his team. Hank's relationship with younger teammates Dusty Baker and Ralph Garr became especially important to him. "Ralph and I felt privileged to be around Hank so much," said Baker. "He taught us how to take care of ourselves—things like how to eat properly. . . . We were all friends, but at the same time Hank was like a father to Ralph and me."

❝All of a sudden they looked up and saw me treading on sacred ground, only a hundred homers away, and they wondered how it was possible. What's Aaron doing here?❞

—HANK ON THE REACTION TO HIS ATTEMPT TO BREAK BABE RUTH'S HOME RUN RECORD

Although Hank was occasionally playing first base to rest his legs a little bit, by April 27 he had hit his 600th career homer. It came off San Francisco Giants pitcher Gaylord Perry. Only

Willie Mays and Ruth were ahead of him now. Hank hit at least seven home runs in every single month of 1971. He ended the season with 47 homers, his highest total ever. And he posted a .327 batting average and drove in 118 runs. At that point, he had 639 career homers.

---

66 *My boy has a chance to do it. He takes care of himself and nothing comes in front of baseball for Henry. Nothing. On days when he is feeling good, it's just too bad for the pitchers.* 99

—ESTELLA AARON, HANK AARON'S MOTHER

Despite Hank's personal life being out of sorts, he was able to keep his famous focus and concentration on his career. Although many people had regarded Willie Mays, who was forty years old, as the successor to Babe Ruth's record, Hank saw the possibility for himself. "It became increasingly obvious that if anybody was going to challenge Ruth's record, it would be me," he said. "I think the press and the fans were reluctant to concede this point, because they had always imagined that a challenger to Ruth would be a charismatic player like Willie or Mickey Mantle—somebody they knew was coming. I had sort of tiptoed along all these years."

For the 1972 season, Hank signed a major contract. The two-year deal made him the first player to earn $200,000 in a season. Yet the Atlanta fans didn't seem happy about it—they seemed resentful and used it as an opportunity to lash out at him, heckling him from the stands and making nasty comments to the star outfielder.

Hank took comfort in the return of his old pal, Eddie Mathews, who was brought on board to manage the Braves. Having Mathews back in his corner was like bringing a bit of the good old days to his present life. "He knew me and understood me as well as anybody in baseball," Hank said.

At age thirty-seven, Hank began hitting home runs at a more regular pace than he ever had in his younger years.

During the 1972 season, Hank's batting average was down and he felt like home runs were the only hits he could manage. On June 10, he hit his 649th homer—a grand slam against Wayne Twitchell of the Phillies. It tied him with Gil Hodges for the National League career grand-slam record (14) and moved Hank past Mays into second place on the all-time home run list. Mays, however, was still playing, so Hank knew that it was possible that Mays could jump back ahead of him in the home run race.

Hank took part in his eighteenth-straight All-Star game on July 25, 1972. The game was held for the first time in Atlanta, and Hank saw yet another chance to impress those Atlanta fans. In all those years, he'd hit only one All-Star game home run. When Hank hit another home run that day, the crowd gave him a standing ovation. "It was one of the best moments I had [in Atlanta]—one of the rare occasions in my career when I felt a little magical," Hank said.

Hank hit another milestone on August 6, when he clobbered home run 660 in a game against the Cincinnati Reds. It broke the record Babe Ruth had established for home runs hit by a player with one team. A month later, Hank broke Stan Musial's all-time record of 6,134 total bases, when he hit two home runs in a game against the Philadelphia Phillies.

❝Hank gave me the best advice I ever got in the big leagues. He said, 'Whatever God gave you, that's what will keep you here.'❞

—BRAVES TEAMMATE RALPH GARR

Hank felt like he had come out from the shadows to suddenly become a celebrity. Although most players would have enjoyed all the attention, Hank wasn't very comfortable with it. The Braves even had to hire a personal secretary to schedule interviews and help sort through the huge amounts of mail he was receiving.

One of Hank's most important interviews was with Billye Williams, who was the cohost of a morning talk show called *Today in Georgia*. A former college English teacher, Billye was a smart and exciting woman. Hank was taken with her, and their friendship eventually turned into romance.

At the end of the 1972 baseball season, Hank had 34 home runs, 77 RBIs, and a .265 batting average. He'd played in the major leagues for eighteen years at that point, and it was his lowest batting average to date.

Billye had previously been married to Sam Williams, a philosophy professor and civil rights activist who died in 1970. From that marriage, Billye had a six-year-old daughter, Ceci, whom Hank adored. He credited Billye with bringing him "into the world of books and ideas." He also joked about his influence on her, saying, "I made her a baseball fan, although she would have me believe that she went to the games for the hot dogs and peanuts."

Hank began using his fame to make a difference. After the 1972 season was over, he hosted a charity bowling tournament to raise money for sickle cell anemia research. Sickle cell anemia is a painful blood disease that typically afflicts people of African descent. He pulled together an all-star guest list of sports stars, including outfielder Reggie Jackson and pitcher Tom Seaver. "It made me proud to think that I could attract all those great people and made me feel good to see them giving up their time for a worthy cause," Hank recalled. "In a way, it was my first tangible dividend for hitting home runs."

Chapter Eight

Tough Times

As Hank Aaron strove to make home run history, he found out that plenty of people wanted to prevent him from doing it. In the early 1970s, as Hank came closer and closer to breaking Babe's record, he began receiving large stacks of vicious hate mail. People wrote comments like, *Everybody loved Babe Ruth. You will be the most hated man in this country if you break his career home run record,* and, *You have the nerve to try to break the Babe's record. 1st of all you're black so you have no business even being here.*

But the letters only made Hank more determined. He later said he liked to imagine that each nasty letter added another home run to his total.

Late in October 1972, Hank's idol Jackie Robinson died. Hank was steadfast in his desire to keep Jackie's dream of equality in baseball alive. "The best way I could do that was to become the all-time home run champion in the history of the game that had kept out black people for more than sixty years," Hank later said. "I owed it to Jackie."

❝As the hate mail piled up, I became more and more intent on breaking the record and shoving it in the ugly faces of those bigots.❞

—HANK AARON

Going into the 1973 season, Hank was only forty-one homers away from reaching Babe Ruth's record. The threatening letters started coming by the truckload. The situation was so serious that the Braves called in the Federal Bureau of Investigation (FBI) to examine the mail. Hank was given a bodyguard, Calvin Wardlaw, to escort him to and from Atlanta Stadium. The FBI was also assigned to look after Hank's parents and children.

"The hardest part about the whole thing was not so much the resentment that I had from outside," Hank explained. "It was the fact that I was separated from my kids. I couldn't do things with my kids, I couldn't go to the park with them, I had to be escorted to different places. My kids had to be sheltered."

Hank's daughter Gaile, then a student at Fisk University in Nashville, was closely watched by the FBI after the agency had heard about a possible kidnapping plot. The college campus was covered with FBI agents. Her friends even had to have mug shots taken, just in case they were suspects. And Gaile's younger siblings were accompanied to school by armed guards.

"My sister, she was about ten or eleven," Gaile recalled. "She said what scared her the most was that if Daddy went on the field and he had his back turned and somebody tried to do something to him and he couldn't defend himself . . . . Now that's a scary thing for a child. I know it was scary for Daddy."

❝When I look back on that whole episode of Henry going after the Ruth record, that's the most amazing part of it to me. People had no idea what he was going through.❞

—Dick Cecil, former vice president of the Braves

While on the road, Hank had to check into hotels under a false name. His teammates would bring food up to his room so that he wouldn't have to go to a restaurant. What should have been a wonderful experience was filled with fear and hatred. "It should have been the most enjoyable time in my life," he later said.

Early in the 1973 season, only about 8,000 fans would show up at home games in Atlanta. But on the road, three times as many fans would show up to see the great Hank Aaron. During games in New York and Los Angeles and Chicago, Hank would get standing ovations. He had the sense that no one in Atlanta cared about what he was doing.

Hank, who had kept his hate-mail situation quiet, finally spoke about it publicly to several sportswriters in May. After the stories appeared in the newspapers, a slew of supportive letters began pouring in. "The encouraging words people wrote helped me fight through the hate," Hank later said.

For years sports fans have been waiting for the right man to come along and break that record. You, Henry Aaron, are that man, read one letter. Another, from a twelve-year-old fan, read: *I wanted to tell you that I have read many articles about the prejudice against you. I really think it's bad. I don't care what color you are. You could be green and it wouldn't matter. . . . It's just some people can't stand to see someone a bit different from them ruin something someone else more like them set.*

Hank Aaron's secretary during his home run chase even began receiving hate mail herself because people were angry that a white woman in the South would work for an African American man.

Hank's secretary, Carla Koplin, had the mammoth task of sorting through his mountains of mail—almost 3,000 letters a day. In fact, in 1973, Hank received 930,000 letters, more than any other U.S. citizen. An address wasn't even necessary to get to him. Letters addressed simply to *Hank Aaron* or his nickname, *The Hammer,* would find their way to Carla.

With all the craziness, Hank wasn't about to back down in the face of adversity in his quest to break the home run record. In 1973 he hit twenty-seven home runs in the first half of the season. His 700th homer came in a game on July 21 against the Philadelphia Phillies' Ken Brett. It rocketed into the stands, 400 feet from home plate. As Hank rounded the bases to reach home plate, he truly felt the weight of his accomplishment. "I was affected in a lot of ways by reaching 700," he recalled. "There was something about getting there that made me feel I was almost at my destination, like I had been traveling on the back roads for twenty years and suddenly I was on Ruth's street, turning onto his driveway."

Then Hank experienced a home run slump, at least by his standards. Ten days passed before Hank hit his 701st homer. More than two weeks after that, Hank hit number 702. That homer tied Stan Musial's all-time record of 1,377 extra-base hits.

With all the excitement of Hank's home run journey, he was constantly surrounded by the press. He began arriving at the ballpark several hours early so that he could nap, undisturbed, in the trainer's room. "The camaraderie of the clubhouse had always been an important part of my baseball life," he said, "and although I realized it wasn't their fault, the news people had taken that away from me. I missed my teammates."

While some people were uneasy about Hank reaching the record, the rest of the world seemed to embrace him. He appeared on the cover of *Newsweek*, he was offered movie and soap opera roles (which he turned down), and he even had songs written about him.

❝*Hank kept almost everything to himself. You couldn't read him because he wouldn't let anything show. It was the same as when he was batting. If he hit a home run or struck out, there was no difference. He would never let the pitcher know how he felt. That was part of his strategy.*❞

—BRAVES TEAMMATE PAUL CASANOVA

Despite all this, Atlanta fans didn't seem to perk up until Hank got closer to hitting his 714th home run. On the night when he hit his 711th home run, there were only 1,362 people in the park, the smallest crowd *ever* in Braves history. On some nights, high school football games in the area attracted larger crowds than the Braves did.

Then, on September 29, the next-to-last day of the season, Hank hit home run number 713. That homer, his fortieth of the season, made the Braves the first team to have three players who hit forty home runs or more in a season. Third baseman Darrell Evans and second baseman Davey Johnson joined Hank in that accomplishment.

On September 30, the final day of the 1973 season, nearly 40,000 fans turned up at Atlanta Stadium hoping to see Hank bash his 714th home run. "I wanted badly to tie the record so it wouldn't be hanging over my head all winter," Hank recalled. "I hated the idea of coming so close and not making it."

In 1973 Hank became the first active player to throw out the first ball at a World Series.

But Hank was also aware that every pitcher he faced was going to do everything in his power to shut him down. It was impossible not to be constantly reminded of Hank's quest. During the last month of the season, when Hank would come up to bat, the umpire would put the game ball in his pocket and throw the pitcher a different one. The Braves had put infrared code numbers on the balls so that Hank's home run souvenirs could be identified afterward.

Houston Astros pitcher Dave Roberts was a formidable opponent for Hank. "I'm not sure I've ever had a battle quite like the one I had with him that day," Hank later said. Hank singled in his first three at bats (tipping his average for the season above .300 for the fourteenth time in his career), but he had no home runs. In the bottom of the eighth inning, he popped out to second base.

When Hank went to take his place in the outfield for the ninth inning, the crowd rose to its feet. They "stood and cheered me for a full five minutes," Hank recalled. "There have been a lot of standing ovations for a lot of baseball players, but this was one for the ages as far as I was concerned. I couldn't believe that I was Hank Aaron and this was Atlanta, Georgia. I thought I'd never see the day."

Willie Mays retired after the 1973 season with 660 career home runs.

Hank would have to put his chase on hold until the start of the 1974 season, but his life certainly wasn't on hold. On

November 12, 1973, in a private ceremony in Jamaica, Hank married Billye. "Billye was a godsend to me, and our marriage really put my life back in order," he revealed. "After being a lost soul for a couple of years, I finally had a home again." Shortly after the wedding, Hank adopted Ceci.

Hank had an extremely busy off-season. He was honored at banquets all over the country, he appeared on TV shows, and celebrities clamored to meet him. But come opening day in 1974, Hank Aaron had only baseball on his mind.

Chapter Nine

Home Run King

Before the 1974 season got under way, Hank found him-self swept up in another controversy. Braves owner Bill Bartholomay met with him and told him they wanted to keep Hank out of the season's first three games in Cincinnati. That way he could tie and break Babe Ruth's record in Atlanta. Hank thought it was a good idea. He said, "I sort of liked the idea of being able to show my grandchildren the spots where 714 and 715 landed."

Hank's Atlanta teammates gave him the nickname "Supe." It was short for "Superstar."

But baseball commissioner Bowie Kuhn was not happy about Bartholomay's plan. He accused the Braves of unsportsmanlike behavior. In response, the Braves agreed to schedule Hank to play two of the three games in Cincinnati. "It was the first and last time I can think of that a player was actually thrown into a game," Hank joked.

On April 4, 1974, forty-year-old Hank arrived at Cincinnati's Riverfront Stadium to face Reds pitcher Jack Billingham. Hank arrived at the ballpark early to announce the creation of the Hank Aaron Scholarship Fund. For every telegram he received after tying or breaking the record (remember, this was the 1970s, long before e-mail), Western Union would contribute one dollar to the fund.

The tension was high that day. Many sportswriters predicted that Hank was going to choke under the pressure of beating Babe Ruth's record. But as the game began, Hank wasn't worried—he was steady and centered. "Pressure never bothered me at home plate because nothing ever bothered me at home plate," he said. "I would be concentrating on the ball in Billingham's hand."

❝There's no greater feeling in sports than the one a player gets when his teammates are genuinely excited over one of his own personal accomplishments.**❞**

—HANK AARON

In the first inning, Hank watched three balls and a strike go by before he whacked a homer into the left-center-field seats. He had done it—he had tied Babe Ruth's record! Hank charged around the bases with tears in his eyes. And he wasn't alone in his excitement. It was mass hysteria all over the field as his teammates pounced on him to congratulate him.

"I just wanted to find home plate somewhere in the middle of the mob that was waiting there, because when I did, the long, excruciating chase would at last be over," Hank later wrote. "I still had one more home run to go to set the record, but for the first time in several long years, I wasn't chasing anybody. It was like I had landed on the moon. . . . All I had to do now was take the next step."

As he reached home plate, Hank savored the fact that his teammates were celebrating his achievement just like it was their own. Then Hank rushed to the stands to hug his father, Herbert, and Billye. Unfortunately, there was no storybook ending to the game. The Braves lost 7–6, in extra innings.

The ball Hank hit for his 714th home run was the first cowhide-ball home run in major league history. Before 1974 the balls were made from horsehide.

In a press conference after the game, with wife Billye at his side, Hank expressed one regret. He'd requested that a moment of silence be held before the game in honor of the sixth anniversary of the assassination of civil rights leader Martin Luther King Jr. That moment never happened.

There was no game the following day, and on Saturday, Hank's pal and manager, Eddie Mathews, benched him. Mathews really wanted Hank's 715th home run to be in Atlanta because he knew how much that would mean to Hank. But Commissioner Kuhn threatened Mathews that if he didn't put Hank in the game on Sunday, he would suspend Mathews. Mathews had no choice but to put Hank in.

In Sunday's game, Hank struck out twice against Reds pitcher Clay Kirby and grounded out a third time. Since the Braves had a solid lead and Hank wasn't hitting well, Mathews took out Hank in the seventh inning and brought in Ralph Garr.

Hank's striking out created a controversy. Some reporters suggested that he struck out on purpose so that he could hit his record-breaking homer in Atlanta. Hank insisted that wasn't true and was angry that people were accusing him of doing so. "I believed in the integrity of the game as strongly as anybody, and it irked me to have my own integrity assaulted," Hank later said.

On April 8, back on his home turf, Hank was ready. It was the season opener at Atlanta Stadium and everyone in the stadium—all 53,775 fans—was waiting to see Hank break Babe Ruth's home run record.

The ballpark had a carnival atmosphere with balloons, cannons, and performances by a drill team. But Hank didn't let anything distract him. During the fourth inning against Los Angeles Dodgers veteran pitcher Al Downing, he finally silenced the naysayers when his 715th home run sailed into baseball history.

When Hank ran the bases for his 715th home run, two college students, Britt Gaston and Cliff Courtney, jumped from the stands and began running alongside Hank.

"I purposely never smiled as I ran the bases after a home run, but I suppose I couldn't help it that time," he recalled. As he reached home plate, teammate Ralph Garr grabbed Hank's leg and tried to plant it on the base, screaming, "Touch it, Supe! Just touch it!"

Hank was relieved that he could put the record behind him. All his struggles, all the criticism, all the hate mail had culminated in this shining moment. And to top it off, the Braves won the game, 7–4.

After the game, Eddie Mathews gathered all of the Braves in the clubhouse and spoke. "I stood up on a table and said what I thought about Hank, which was that he was the best ballplayer I ever saw in my life," he recalled.

Hank was the new home run king. And more than 35 million TV viewers and radio listeners had experienced the moment right along with him. Hank's achievement made front-page news across the globe. One Japanese newspaper's headline was, "White Ball Dances Through Atlanta's White Mist." A sportswriter for the Mexican newspaper *El Sol de Mexico* wrote, "We lived through this historic moment, the most fabulous in the world. Thanks to God we witnessed this moment of history."

❝I was no longer Henry Aaron of Mobile, Alabama— husband, father, private person, outfielder, fastball hitter, fish eater, blues fan; I was the home run king.**❞**

—HANK AARON

The next day, Hank found 20,000 telegrams—many of them positive—waiting for him in the office. He learned that a baby in Iowa was named Aaron Black in his honor.

Hank quickly realized that his accomplishment would change his life forever. "I would never against be just another ballplayer who went to the park, took his times at bat, showered, and went home," he said. "For better or for worse, I had to learn to live with that, because it would be that way for the rest of my life."

Yet the day after Hank's 715th home run, it wasn't even the lead headline in the city's paper. Two days after Hank made history, only 6,500 fans turned up to watch the Braves play. The situation made Hank realize that his time in Atlanta had come to a close. He let the Braves know that 1974 would be his final season with them, and in July, they held a day in his honor during which he received a Cadillac and other lavish gifts.

Hank was also given farewell ceremonies at every National League ballpark. He said that the most memorable event took place in New York City. He met Claire Ruth (Babe's widow) and Eleanor Gehrig (widow of famous Yankee Lou Gehrig) at City Hall and then rode up to Harlem to speak to a large crowd. He called it a high point of his career.

❝When he joined the club, the first thing I did with him was to sit down with him and pick his brain. I asked him what he attributed all his good years to, year in and year out, and he said one word: concentration.❞

—MILWAUKEE BREWERS TEAMMATE GEORGE SCOTT

In Hank's final game with the Braves, only 11,000 people showed up at Atlanta Stadium. Hank felt hurt "to know that so few cared enough to buy a ticket for my last of 3,076 games over twenty-one years with the Braves," he said. He hit his twentieth homer of the season and said good-bye to the Braves. But he wasn't ready to give up on baseball quite yet.

On November 1, Hank met another legend—Japanese baseball's home run king Sadaharu Oh. At Tokyo's Korakuen Stadium, 50,000 fans flocked to watch the two heroes slug it out for home run supremacy. Hank defeated Oh, 10 home runs to 9.

The following day, while he was still in Japan, Hank got a call that would eventually take him back home. Milwaukee Brewers owner Bud Selig told him that he'd been traded to the four-year-old team. He'd return to the city where he started his major league career. It was great news. "I knew I was going to a place where I was wanted, and that sounded awfully good," he said. His contract was for $240,000 a year for two years.

For the first time in his major league career, Hank would be in the American League. For the past twenty years, Hank spent every season facing National League pitchers. He knew the pitchers' quirks and habits. In switching leagues, he'd have to overcome the obstacle of not knowing the strengths and weaknesses of his opponents.

Almost 48,000 Brewers fans showed up to welcome Hammerin' Hank on opening day, April 18, 1975. They even serenaded him with a version of "Hello, Dolly," and sang, "Hello,

Henry. . . . It's so nice to have you back where you belong."

Playing as a designated hitter, forty-one-year-old Hank broke Babe Ruth's record of 2,211 runs batted in on May 1. Yet by the end of the season, his average only hit .234 and he had 12 home runs. "I was sluggish and inconsistent," he admitted.

LICENSE TO HIT

A designated hitter (Hank's final position with the Brewers) is a hitter who bats in place of the pitcher. A DH doesn't play the field—he sits on the bench when he isn't batting. The DH is used only in the American League, where the position was established in 1973.

Determined to make the most of his contract, Hank headed into the 1976 season with conviction. "I convinced myself that I was not a .234 hitter, that I didn't want to go out that way. I thought I could turn things around if I rededicated myself," he later said.

But when Hank continued to struggle in 1976, he resolved that the season would be his last as a major leaguer. "There was no mistaking it this time—I couldn't go on another year. I knew it was over when I couldn't hit consistently in batting practice," he said.

But the year still held a few highlights for Hank. In the tenth inning of a game against the Texas Rangers in July, Hank's home run helped the Brewers beat the Rangers. That win gave the team a sweep of the four-game series. "The fans were so charged up that they called me out of the clubhouse for a standing ovation. That's the way I like to remember Milwaukee," said Hank. "At the age of forty-two, every home run took on a little extra meaning to me." On July 20, in a home game against the California Angels, he slammed home run 755, the final bomb of his career.

In September the Brewers held Hank Aaron Day at County Stadium. It was Hank's official retirement party. At the event, the Brewers retired his number and established a showcase of memorabilia from Hank's career. Hank declared that he'd donate one of his most prized possessions for the showcase—the shower shoes he'd worn for the past twenty-two years!

On September 3, 1977, Sadaharu Oh hit his 756th home run to become the most prolific slugger in international baseball history.

On October 3, Hank played in his final major league game. It was his 3,298th game and he went to bat for the 12,364th time (both figures making baseball history). In his final game, which was held in Detroit, he hit a ground ball for a single. It was his 3,771st hit and his 2,297th RBI. He wound up tied with Babe Ruth for second in runs scored with 2,174, trailing Ty Cobb by 71. "I sort of liked the idea of sharing something with Ruth," he noted.

As Hank trotted off the field, a big smile spread across his face. It might have been the end of his playing career, but it wouldn't be the end of Hank Aaron's legacy.

❝There's nothing I can do that's more important than what I can do for children—black and white, but especially black. If the home run record gives me more power to inspire children—and I know that it does— then the ordeal was worth every moment of sleep I lost and every hurt I felt from every hate letter.❞

—HANK AARON

Doing the Right Thing

Before he officially retired as a player, Hank Aaron announced that he would be returning to the Braves—but this time as a player development director. He would help to scout young talent in the organization's farm system. "Despite my strained relationship with Atlanta—and as much as I loved Milwaukee—deep down I was a Southerner, and I was prepared to go back," he explained.

Hank had an opportunity to flourish in this arena. The position would allow Hank to be a mentor, a role his idol Jackie Robinson had once played for him.

Importantly, the job was a chance for Hank to have a say in creating greater racial equality in baseball, something he'd always wanted to do. "I don't know what role, if any, baseball might have had in store for me if [Braves owner Ted Turner] hadn't come along with the Braves job," Hank later said.

Hank was even offered the position of team manager several times by Turner in the late 1970s, but he turned him down. Hank worried that he was too busy for the job: "I would have some conflicts with a job that's so demanding on my time. I make a lot of speeches and charity appearances and do a lot of business traveling, and I wouldn't want to give up any of that." In his role with the Braves at that time, he was the highest-ranking African American executive in baseball.

On August 1, 1982, Hank reached another milestone in his career when he was inducted into the Baseball Hall of Fame. He was elected nine votes short of unanimous. (Only Ty Cobb received a higher percentage of votes cast.) Hank's wife, Billye, and his children all attended the ceremony. Hank's brother Tommie, who'd once been his teammate on the Milwaukee Braves, was by his side to witness the proud day. Sadly, Tommie died later that year from leukemia.

Hank said that being inducted into the Baseball Hall of Fame was one of the most satisfying moments of his career. During his speech, he talked about how Jackie Robinson had paved the way for him as a player. He said that his presence in the Hall of Fame "proved that a man's ability is limited only by his lack of opportunity." He also pointed out that he'd never sought fame as a player—he'd only wanted to make the most of his talents on the field.

And around that time, a group of Atlanta residents formed a committee to erect a statue of Hank in front of Atlanta Stadium, commemorating his 715th home run. "It was an undertaking that flattered and humbled me and also embarrassed me a little before it was finished," Hank recalled. "In the end, I was profoundly grateful that it was done."

Through the 1980s, Hank continued to use his celebrity to speak out against bigotry in baseball. It made him a target for criticism, but he was a mouthpiece for the black baseball players who had come before him. "I was trying to carve out a role as some sort of leader, trying to do and say things that would make a difference." In the 1990s, he became a senior vice president for the Braves.

Hank has also devoted time to civil rights organizations and charities. He is on the executive boards of the National Association for the Advancement of Colored People, Big Brothers/Big Sisters, and Rainbow/PUSH Coalition, founded by Reverend Jesse Jackson to create social, racial, and economic justice. He's also helped raise millions of dollars for the Hank Aaron Scholarship Fund. With his former home run rival Sadaharu Oh, he helped establish a program to promote baseball in developing countries. Hank and Billye also created the Chasing the Dream Foundation to help youngsters in Atlanta and Milwaukee.

On February 5, 1999, Hank celebrated his sixty-fifth birthday. That year he was honored for his achievements as a player and as a person with the establishment of the Hank Aaron Award. It recognizes the top National League and American League players with a combination of five offensive abilities—home runs, RBIs, stolen bases, runs scored, and batting average. "This award says that I wasn't just a home run hitter," Hank declared. "I was able to do something else in baseball. I won two batting titles, I was able to field my position, run the bases. I batted in a lot of runs. I would like people to realize that." Hank was also named to the All-Century Team, securing him yet another place in baseball history.

These days, the man who finished his career with a lifetime average of .305 and averaged 33 homers and 100 RBIs per year enjoys quiet time with his family at home in an Atlanta suburb. He no longer plays baseball. "Tennis is my sport now," he commented. "After I retired, I tried playing on a softball team, but I couldn't hit the big, slow thing. Tennis is the game that makes you feel like you're really playing something, and I love every minute of it."

Hank knows he'll be forever associated with the sport he started playing as a scrawny youngster back in Toulminville, Alabama. "Baseball needs me because it needs somebody to stir the pot, and I need it because it's my life," he explained.

"It's the means I have to make a little difference in the world."

Hank Aaron still hasn't stopped in his pursuit for social justice. "I once read a quote from Jackie [Robinson] that speaks for me too. He said, 'Life owes me nothing. Baseball owes me nothing. But I cannot as an individual rejoice in the good things I have been permitted to work for and learn while the humblest of my brothers is down in the deep hole hollering for help and not being heard.' All I can add to that is, Amen."

PERSONAL STATISTICS

Name:

Henry Louis Aaron

Nicknames:

Hank, Hammerin' Hank, The Hammer, Bad Henry, Supe

Born:

February 5, 1934

Height:

6'0"

Weight:

190 lbs.

Batted:

Right

Threw:

Right

BATTING STATISTICS

Year	Team	Avg	G	AB	Runs	Hits	2B	3B	HR	RBI	SB
1954	MLN	.280	122	468	58	131	27	6	13	69	2
1955	MLN	.314	153	602	105	189	37	9	27	106	3
1956	MLN	.328	153	609	106	200	34	14	26	92	2
1957	MLN	.322	151	615	118	198	27	6	44	132	1
1958	MLN	.326	153	601	109	196	34	4	30	95	4
1959	MLN	.355	154	629	116	223	46	7	39	123	8
1960	MLN	.292	153	590	102	172	20	11	40	126	16
1961	MLN	.327	155	603	115	197	39	10	34	120	21
1962	MLN	.323	156	592	127	191	28	6	45	128	15
1963	MLN	.319	161	631	121	201	29	4	44	130	31
1964	MLN	.328	145	570	103	187	30	2	24	95	22
1965	MLN	.318	150	570	109	181	40	1	32	89	24
1966	ATL	.279	158	603	117	168	23	1	44	127	21
1967	ATL	.307	155	600	113	184	37	3	39	109	17
1968	ATL	.287	160	606	84	174	33	4	29	86	28
1969	ATL	.300	147	547	100	164	30	3	44	97	9
1970	ATL	.298	150	516	103	154	26	1	38	118	9
1971	ATL	.327	139	495	95	162	22	3	47	118	1
1972	ATL	.265	129	449	75	119	10	0	34	77	4
1973	ATL	.301	120	392	84	118	12	1	40	96	1
1974	ATL	.268	112	340	47	91	16	0	20	69	1
1975	MIL	.234	137	465	45	109	16	2	12	60	0
1976	MIL	.229	85	271	22	62	8	0	10	35	0
	Total	.305	3298	12364	2174	3771	624	98	755	2297	240

Key: Avg: batting average; G: games; AB: at bats; 2B: doubles; 3B: triples; HR: home runs; RBI: runs batted in; SB: stolen bases

FIELDING STATISTICS

Year	Team	Pos	G	C	PO	A	E	DP	FLD%
1954	MLN	OF	116	235	223	5	7	0	.970
1955	MLN	OF	126	272	254	9	9	2	.967
		2B	27	176	86	84	6	23	.966
1956	MLN	OF	152	346	316	17	13	4	.962
1957	MLN	OF	150	361	346	9	6	0	.983
1958	MLN	OF	153	322	305	12	5	0	.984
1959	MLN	OF	152	278	261	12	5	3	.982
		3B	5	12	2	10	0	0	1.000
1960	MLN	OF	153	339	320	13	6	6	.982
		2B	2	1	1	0	0	0	1.000
1961	MLN	OF	154	397	377	13	7	3	.982
		3B	2	4	2	2	0	0	1.000
1962	MLN	OF	153	358	340	11	7	1	.980
		1B	1	1	1	0	0	0	1.000
1963	MLN	OF	161	283	267	10	6	1	.979
1964	MLN	OF	139	288	270	13	5	5	.983
		2B	11	30	14	15	1	2	.967
1965	MLN	OF	148	311	298	9	4	2	.987
1966	ATL	OF	158	331	315	12	4	5	.988
		2B	2	0	0	0	0	0	0.000
1967	ATL	OF	152	340	321	12	7	3	.979
		2B	1	1	1	0	0	0	1.000
1968	ATL	OF	151	346	330	13	3	2	.991
		1B	14	97	88	7	2	8	.979

FIELDING STATISTICS (continued)

Year	Team	Pos	G	C	PO	A	E	DP	FLD%
1969	ATL	OF	144	283	267	11	5	3	.982
		1B	4	34	32	2	0	3	1.000
1970	ATL	OF	125	258	246	6	6	1	.977
	ATL	1B	11	78	73	4	1	6	.987
1971	ATL	1B	71	670	629	38	3	56	.996
		OF	60	108	104	2	2	0	.981
1972	ATL	1B	109	1048	968	66	14	79	.987
		OF	15	35	28	4	3	0	.914
1973	ATL	OF	105	216	206	5	5	0	.977
1974	ATL	OF	89	147	142	3	2	0	.986
1975	MIL	DH	128	-	-	-	-	-	-
		OF	3	2	2	0	0	0	1.000
1976	MIL	DH	74	-	-	-	-	-	-
		OF	1	1	1	0	0	0	1.000
	Total		3020	8009	7436	429	144	218	.982

Key: Pos: position; G: games; C: chances (balls hit to a position); PO: putouts; A: assists; E: errors; DP: double plays; FLD%: fielding percentage

SOURCES

2 Hank Aaron with Lonnie Wheeler, *I Had a Hammer: The Hank Aaron Story* (New York: HarperCollins, 1991), 370.

2 Ibid., 371.

3 Ibid.

3 Ibid., 373.

5 Ibid., 11.

6 Ibid., 12.

6 Ibid., 17.

7 Ibid., 16.

8 Ibid., 18.

10 Ibid., 30.

10 James Takach, *Hank Aaron* (New York: Chelsea House Publishers, 1992), 18.

11 Rennert, *Henry Aaron*, 25.

12 Aaron, *I Had a Hammer*, 32.

12 Ibid., 33.

13-14 Ibid.

14 Ibid., 34.

14 Ibid.

15 Ibid.

16 Ibid., 35.

17 Richard Scott Rennert, *Henry Aaron* (New York: Chelsea House Publishers, 1993), 32.

17 Ibid., 34.

18 Ibid.

18 Ibid.

19 Aaron, *I Had a Hammer*, 54.

19–20 Ibid., 57.

21 Ibid., 48.

21–22 Rennert, *Henry Aaron*, 40–41.

22 Ibid., 43.

23 Aaron, *I Had a Hammer*, 78.

23 Ibid., 109.

26 Takach, *Hank Aaron*, 29.

26 Aaron, *I Had a Hammer*, 120.

27 Ibid.

27 Ibid., 122.

30 Ibid., 146.

30 Ibid., 154.

30 Ibid., 157.

31 Ibid., 145.

32 Rennert, *Henry Aaron*, 55.

32 Aaron, *I Had a Hammer*, 153.

37 Ibid., 169.

37 Ibid., 177.

38 Sandy Tolan, *Me and Hank: A Boy and His Hero*, Twenty-Five Years Later (New York: Free Press, 2000), 105.

39 Aaron, *I Had a Hammer*, 179.

39 Ibid., 183.

40 Ibid.

41 Ibid., 186.

41 Rennert, *Henry Aaron*, 77.

41 Ibid., 77.

42 Aaron, *I Had a Hammer*, 195.

42 Ibid., 197.

43 Rennert, *Henry Aaron*, 84.

43 Aaron, *I Had a Hammer*, 219.

44 Ibid., 224.

44 Ibid., 221.

44 Ibid., 223.

46 Ibid., 219.

46 Rennert, *Henry Aaron*, 88.

47 Aaron, *I Had a Hammer*, 227.

47 Ibid., 233.

47 Ibid.

48 Ibid., 230.

48 Ibid., 232.

49 Ibid., 231.

49–50 Ibid., 239–240.

50 Ibid., 240.

51 Ibid., 241.

51 Ibid., 240–241.

52 Ibid., 245.

53–54 Ibid., 249.

54 Ibid., 248.

55–56 Ibid., 252.

56 Ibid., 257.

56 Ibid., 258.

56 Ibid., 259.

57 Rennert, *Henry Aaron*, 95.

57 Aaron, *I Had a Hammer*, 261.

57 Ibid., 264.

57–58 Ibid.

58 Ibid., 260.

58 Ibid., 270–271.

59 Ibid., 272.

59 Ibid.

60 Ibid., 274.

60–61 Ibid., 280–281.

62 Ibid., 285.

63 Takach, *Hank Aaron*, 48.

63 Aaron, *I Had a Hammer*, 288.

64 Ibid., 287.
64 Ibid., 291–292.
65 Takach, *Hank Aaron*, 49.
65 Aaron, *I Had a Hammer: The Hank Aaron Story*, 292–293.
65 Ibid., 294.
66 "Hank Aaron: Quotations From and About Hank Aaron," *baseball -almanac.com*, n.d., http://www .baseball-almanac.com/quotes/ quoaar.shtml (May 3, 2005).
66 Aaron, *I Had a Hammer*, 294.
67 Ibid., 328–329.
68 Ibid., 300.
68 Ibid., 302.
69–70 Ibid., 305.
70 Ibid., 306.
71 Rennert, *Henry Aaron*, 104.
71–72 Aaron, *I Had a Hammer*, 309.
72 Ibid., 321.
72 Tolan, *Me and Hank*, 34–35.
73 Ibid., 55.
73 Aaron, *I Had a Hammer*, 327.
73 Rennert, *Henry Aaron*, 106.
74 Aaron, *I Had a Hammer*, 321.
74 Ibid., 332.
75 Ibid., 341.
76 Ibid.
76 Ibid., 329–331.
77 Ibid., 346.
78 Ibid., 347–348.
78 Ibid., 349.
79 Ibid., 351.
80 Ibid., 354.
81 Ibid., 355.
81 Ibid., 357.
81 Ibid., 361.
82 Ibid.
83 Ibid., 365–366.
84 Ibid., 370.
84 Ibid., 371.
85 Ibid., 372.
85 Ibid., 376.
85 Rennert, *Henry Aaron*, 111.
85–86 Aaron, *I Had a Hammer*, 376–377.
86 Ibid., 401.
86–87 Ibid., 394.
87 Ibid., 398.
88 Ibid., 403.
88 Ibid., 406.
88 Ibid., 408.
89 Ibid., 409.
90 Ibid., 413.
90 Ibid., 381.
91 Ibid., 411.
91 Ibid., 423.
92 Ibid., 424.
92 Ibid., 436.
93 Ibid., 439, 441.
93 Ibid., 438–439.
94 William Ladson, "Q&A with Hank Aaron," *SportingNews.com*, April 8, 1999, http://www.sportingnews .com/archives/aaron/152544.html (May 3, 2005).
94 Aaron, *I Had a Hammer*, 454–455.
94–95 Ibid., 456.
95 Aaron, *I Had a Hammer*, 457.

BIBLIOGRAPHY

Books

Aaron, Hank, with Lonnie Wheeler. *I Had a Hammer: The Hank Aaron Story.* New York: HarperCollins, 1991.

Honig, Donald. *The Power Hitters.* St. Louis, MO: The Sporting News, 1989.

Rennert, Richard Scott. *Henry Aaron.* New York: Chelsea House Publishers, 1993.

Ribowsky, Mark. *A Complete History of the Negro Leagues, 1884–1955.* New York: Birch Lane Press, 1995.

Stanton, Tom. *Hank Aaron and the Home Run That Changed America.* New York: William Morrow, 2004.

Takach, James. *Hank Aaron.* New York: Chelsea House Publishers, 1992.

Tolan, Sandy. *Me and Hank: A Boy and His Hero, Twenty-Five Years Later.* New York: Free Press, 2000.

Zoss, Joel and John S. Bowman. *The History of Major League Baseball.* New York: Crescent Books, 1992.

Selected Magazine and Online Articles

"A Prisoner of Memory." *Sports Illustrated,* December 7, 1992, 80.

Ladson, William. "Q&A with Hank Aaron." *The Sporting News,* April 8, 1999.

Minshew, Wayne. "Aaron's 10 Favorite Homers." *The Sporting News,* February 10, 1973.

Schwartz, Larry. "Hank Aaron: Hammerin' Back at Racism." *ESPN.com.* n.d. http://espn.go.com/sportscentury/features/00006764.html (April 5, 2005).

WEBSITES

Baseball Library

http://www.baseballlibrary.com/baseballlibrary/ballplayers/A/Aaron_Hank.stm

This online baseball encyclopedia has a section dedicated to Hank's career, including a timeline of his achievements.

The National Baseball Hall of Fame: The Official Site

http://www.baseballhalloffame.org/hofers_and_honorees/hofer_bios/aaron_hank.htm

This is a great resource for Hank Aaron's stats and facts.

The Sporting News

http://www.sportingnews.com/archives/aaron/

The sports magazine has a section full of information on Hank's career, including photos and interviews with the legendary ballplayer.

INDEX